P9-AQH-802

HIRAM HALLE MEMORIAL LIBRARY
271 Westchester Avenue
Pound Ridge, New York
10576-1714

The <u>most</u> <u>excellent</u> book of
how to be a
juggler

Mitch Mitchelson

Illustrated by Rob Shone and Peter Harper

DISCARD

Copper Beech Books
Brookfield, Connecticut

11/98 B+T

J
793.8
M

HIRAM HALL MEMORIAL LIBRARY

© Aladdin Books Ltd
1997
© U.S. text 1997

Designed and produced by
Aladdin Books Ltd
28 Percy Street
London
WIP 0LD

First published in the
United States in 1997 by
Copper Beech Books,
an imprint of
The Millbrook Press
2 Old New Milford Road
Brookfield, Connecticut
06084

Editor
Sarah Levete
Design
David West Children's
Book Design
Designer
Simon Morse
Picture research
Brooks Krikler Research
Illustrators
Rob Shone and Peter Harper

Printed in Belgium
All rights reserved
5 4 3 2 1

Library of Congress Cataloging-
in-Publication Data
Mitchelson, Mitch
How to be a Juggler / Mitch
Mitchelson ; illustrated by
Rob Shone and Peter Harper
p. cm. Includes index.
ISBN 0-7613-0618-8 (lib. bdg.)
— ISBN 0-7613-0632-3 (pbk.)
1. Juggling I. Title II. Series
GV1558.M58 1997   97-8012
793.8'7—dc21   CIP

CONTENTS

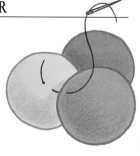

INTRODUCTION

Juggling is catching! Catch some juggling balls, and you won't want to stop. There are pictures dating back to 1900 B.C. of women juggling balls in ancient Egypt. In ancient Rome, jugglers threw rounded stones, torches, and shields into the air. The French word for juggler, "jongleur," was used to describe wandering performers from jesters to jugglers *(left)*, in the Middle Ages. Today, you can see jugglers performing street theater. Join the fun here – start juggling.

As you read the book, look for these symbols:
★ *shows you how to make your juggling props and gives you basic tips on juggling techniques.*
✔ *gives hints on how to perfect your juggling performance and suggestions for more advanced juggling.*

Remember that juggling takes a lot of practice, so be patient. It's worth it!

Tools of the TRADE

Make your own juggling balls... from a pair of old socks!

Start your juggling practice with round, soft objects, from rolled up socks to hand-made juggling balls. These are good to begin with because they don't bounce everywhere when you drop them. When you are confident juggling with balls, try juggling with clubs *(see page 18).*

★ *For two juggling balls you will need: a pair of socks; a filling of lentils, rice, or pearl barley (for juggling inside) or plastic beads (for juggling outside); scissors; fabric paint; sequins; and needle and thread.*

1 Cut off the end of the foot piece from an old sock.

2 Stitch around the hole in the foot piece, leaving a gap for your filling. Leave some thread free. Pour in your filling.

Foot piece

3 Pull the thread in and knot tightly enough to prevent your filling from falling out.

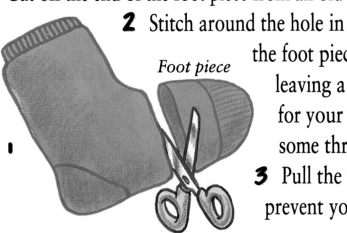

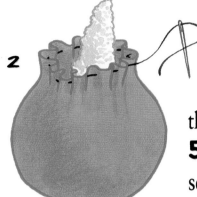

4 Cut out a small square from the left-over piece of sock. Sew it in place over the knot on your juggling ball.

5 Paint the ball or sew on some sequins. Repeat for the second ball.

Make your own juggling clubs

1 Stuff a plastic bottle loosely with colored material and/or colored paper.

2 Place the wooden baton into the bottle. Leave the handle poking out.

3 Ask an adult to help you screw the baton or stick to the base of the bottle.

4 Ask an adult to help you screw a piece of rubber to the end of the handle.

5 Put some wrapping or wadding around the end of the handle so that it is not too hard to catch.

6 Decorate brightly! Repeat for the second club.

★ *For two clubs you will need: two similar empty plastic bottles; colored material or paper; two long wooden batons or sticks; four screws; and two pieces of rubber such as doorstops.*

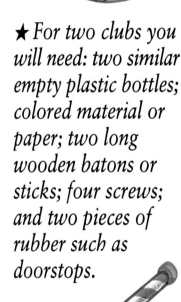

Useful TIPS

Learning to juggle is fun, but you need to practice.

It's hard to juggle if you are tense and angry!

Relax!

Give your shoulders and wrists a shake to release any tension. Juggle with your juggling objects at waist level; catch them at chest level. Try not to raise your hands to catch the objects at shoulder level.

It's easier to juggle when you are relaxed.

What to wear... and where to do it!

Loose-fitting or stretchable clothes will help keep your arms and legs free while you juggle. They are also more comfortable when you need to pick up dropped objects. To begin with, practice over the bed – it will save you from picking up your juggling balls from the floor. Watch out for any breakables or even any precious family heirlooms. Give yourself plenty of room!

Practice throwing and catching one ball.

3

I Extend your forearms in front of you, at waist level. Keep your elbows at your side. Hold one ball in your hand. Imagine two points in the air. One is above your right hand; the other is above your left hand. They are both level with the top of your head.

2 Toss the ball to the point above the throwing hand; catch it with the same hand. Repeat throwing and catching with your other hand.

4

3 Throw the ball in your right hand to the point above your left hand. Catch it with your left hand. Repeat throwing with your left hand and catching with your right hand.

4 Sway from foot to foot as you toss the ball from hand to hand.

5 Throw the ball under your leg *(left)*, or over your shoulder!

outside

inside

5

"Inside" means the ball passes inside, or under, another ball. "Outside" means the ball passes outside, or over, another ball (right).

Juggling with two BALLS

Your basic two-ball juggling technique.

1 Hold one ball in each hand. Throw the ball in your right hand to a spot above your left hand, at eye level. As the ball reaches its peak, and just before it begins to fall, release the ball from your left hand.
2 Throw this ball to a point just above eye level, over your right hand. Catch the first ball in your left hand; catch the second ball in your right hand.

✓ *If you have difficulty juggling with balls, practice, or even perform (see pages 23-24), with scarves.*

★ *Left-handed jugglers!* ★
Swap left for right in all the instructions.

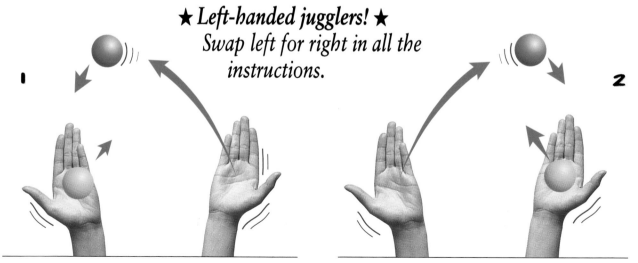

Circles and COLUMNS

Now for two one-handed tricks!

1 For a one-handed two-ball column *(right)* take two balls in one hand. Imagine two parallel lines or columns from your hand to points just above eye level. Toss the first ball along the inside column to this level. As it reaches its peak, move your hand across to toss the second ball along the outside column.

2 Catch the first ball as the second ball reaches its peak. Continue the sequence.

Two ball column

For one-handed tricks, keep the hand that is not juggling out of the way!

Two-ball circle

1 For a one-handed two-ball circle *(left)* take two balls in one hand. Throw one ball up and to the outside, in a clockwise arc. When the ball reaches its peak, throw the second ball in the same direction.

2 When the second ball is at its highest point, catch the first ball. Continue the sequence in a clockwise arc or circle.

Three-ball JUGGLING

The cascade is the basic juggling pattern.

★ *When you begin juggling with three balls, it will help your juggling if you identify each ball by a letter of the alphabet, as shown in the instructions for each trick.*

1 Take two balls in your right hand and one ball in your left hand. Think of the balls in your right hand as A and C and the ball in your left hand as B.

2 Throw ball A from your right hand to the imaginary point above your left hand.

3 As it reaches its highest point, toss ball B from your left hand inside to the imaginary point above your right hand.

4 Catch ball A with your left hand.

5 As ball B reaches its full height, throw ball C from your right hand, inside to the point above your left hand.

6 Catch ball B with your right hand.

7 As ball C hits its peak, throw ball A from your left hand to the point above your right hand. Catch ball C in your left hand. Continue the sequence.

8 Count how many throws you do before you drop a ball. Challenge yourself by trying to beat your record.

The three-ball cascade pattern follows a figure eight pattern (right). *Each throw should be the same height.*

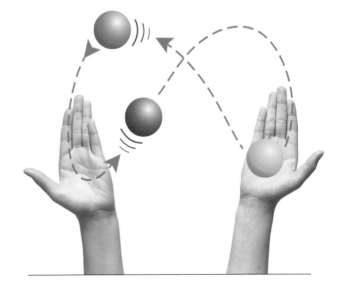

★ *Concentrate on the objects that you are juggling at their peak in the air – try not to look at your hands.*

Three-ball TRICKERY

Now you've conquered the cascade – continue the challenge!

1

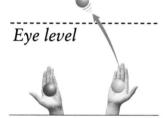

Eye level

2

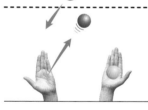

3

4

Juggle with one ball higher than the other *(left)*.

1 Take two balls in your right hand (balls A and C); and one in your left hand (ball B).

2 Throw ball A in the cascade pattern *(see page 10)*, to a point at well above eye level, over your left hand.

3 Throw ball B to eye level, above your right hand.

4 Throw ball C from your right hand, to just above eye level, above your left hand. Catch ball A in your left hand. Catch ball B in your right hand. Catch ball C in your left hand.

Juggle one over the top *(right)*.

1 Begin a three-ball cascade.

2 Throw the ball which you have caught **outside** the returning ball, not inside.

3 Resume a cascade, or toss every ball over the top.

1   **2**

A swift under arm pass

❙ Start by juggling a three-ball cascade. Throw one of the balls you catch under your opposite arm. Your arms momentarily cross. Resume the cascade.

Pass one arm under the other.

Planets around the sun

❙ With one hand, throw two balls (A and B) in a clockwise circle *(see page 9)* with your right hand or a counterclockwise circle with your left hand.

2 Hold ball C in your other hand. Circle ball C around your head at the same time as you juggle balls A and B. This trick creates an image of planets circling the sun.

Ball C stays in your hand.

✔ *Why not give your audience a lesson in astronomy at the same time as stunning them with your juggling performance?*

More three-ball TRICKERY

Tricks with which to trick your audience!

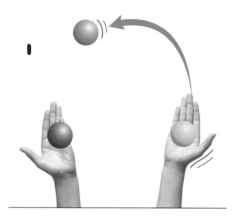

Reverse cascade

★ *Reverse the cascade pattern (see pages 10-11). Instead of throwing the balls outside each other, throw them inside each other (see page 7).*

1 Hold two balls in your right hand (balls A and C) and one in your left hand (ball B). From your right hand, throw ball A in an arc shape to its imaginary point above your left hand.

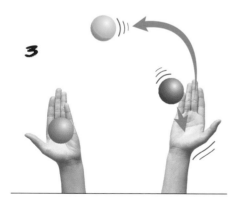

2 From your left hand, throw ball B outside ball A, to an imaginary point just above your right hand.

3 As ball B drops, throw ball C (from your right hand) outside and over the falling ball B.

4 Continue the cycle.

Three-ball trickery juggling with... two balls!

I Begin a column with two balls (A and B) in one hand *(see page 9)*. Hold the third ball (ball C) in your other hand. Move it up and down in a straight line.

2 As you juggle your column, you are holding rather than throwing ball C.

✔ *This pretend move will definitely raise a laugh – and maybe even some applause!*

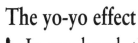

The yo-yo effect

I In one hand, throw two balls (A and B) in a column *(see page 9)*.

2 Hold ball C in your other hand. Hold ball C above ball A on the inside column.

3 Continue to juggle your column; keep following ball A with ball C. It is as if there is an invisible string connecting the two balls.

Four, five, and nine BALLS!

Feeling adventurous? Try juggling with more and more balls.

The balls do not cross each other.

2

Four-ball juggling is based on two balls in each hand moving in a circular pattern *(see page 8)* – you use both hands at the same time! Left-handed jugglers – don't swap left for right here!

1 In your right hand, juggle two balls (A and B) in a clockwise direction.

2 In your left hand, juggle the other two balls (C and D) in a counterclockwise direction. Throw ball A from your right hand before you throw ball C from your left hand.

✔ *Want to juggle with numbers? How about nine balls? Stick, glue or sew three balls together. Make three sets. Juggle the sets as a three-ball cascade. Bravo! You are now a nine-ball juggler!*

From cheating with nine to juggling with five!

Rome was not built in a day! And the same applies to five-ball juggling. You need lots of patience and many

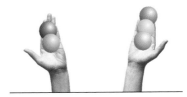

months practice! So here goes.

1 Take three balls in your right hand and two balls in your left hand. The balls in your right hand are A, C, and E. The balls in your left hand are B and D. Raise the height of your imaginary points by two feet to give yourself plenty of room.

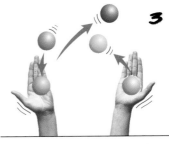

2 Throw ball A to its high imaginary point above the left hand. As it is just over halfway through its journey, throw ball B inside ball A to the point above your right hand.

3 As ball B passes its halfway point, throw ball C inside it.

4 Throw ball D inside ball C as ball C passes its halfway point. Catch ball A in your left hand. Toss ball E inside ball D just as ball D crosses its halfway mark.

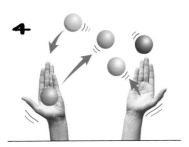

5 Catch balls B and D in your right hand. Catch balls C and E in your left hand.

6 Throw ball A and repeat the pattern! Good luck!

Club JUGGLING

Time for a change! Try some juggling with clubs.

1 Practice with one club. Hold it in your hand by the handle. Throw it in the air so that it spins once before you catch it again by the handle.

2 Toss it in the same way from hand to hand.

3 Try a cascade with two balls and one club.

4 Now try the three-club cascade. The pattern is the same as for the three-ball cascade. Each club has to spin once through the air between throwing and catching.

★ *Your wrists control the spin and your arms control the height – you need plenty of height for the clubs to spin and rotate.*

Club trickery
For a double spin, spin one of the clubs with a little more force and flick – this will make the club rotate twice in the air before you catch the handle.

Cane TRICKERY

Pick up a cane!

Hold the cane between your thumb and index finger. Spin or walk it around each finger *(above)*. "Walk" it backward and forward.

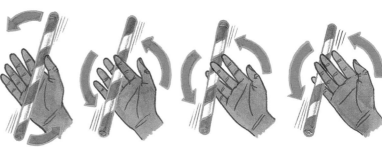

★ *Keep the cane far away from your eyes.*

1 Bend your elbow with your arm out to the side. Hold the middle of the cane between your thumb and index finger. Rest one end of it in the crook of your arm. Lift the other end of the cane toward your shoulder by bringing your arm into your side.

Use the same arm for each step.

2 Let the cane slip through your fingers.

3 Quickly turn your arm under and behind to catch the cane.

1

2

3

Hat ROUTINES

Say "hello" or "thank you" to your audience with a hat trick.

★ *You will need: 2 large circles of black cardboard; a wide rectangle of black cardboard; scissors; masking tape; stars and glitter.*

❶ Cut a hole in one circle. Make sure that the hole is big enough to fit onto your head.

2 Cut slits inside the hole and on the outside of the other circle; fold them into flaps.

3 Roll the rectangular cardboard into a tube and tape the edges.

4 Tape the flaps of each circle to the inside of the tube. Decorate your hat with stars and glitter.

Hat off with one hand

❶ Wearing your hat, reach over to the back of your head. Grab the hat with your fingers on the top of the brim and your thumb underneath.

2 Lift the hat off, turning it over between your index finger and thumb.

3 Turn the hat until your arm is fully extended.

4 Reverse the move to return the hat to your head. It will appear to your audience as if the hat has rolled back up your arm onto your head.

Hat off with two hands

1 Use both hands. On either side of the hat, place your thumbs on top of the brim. Put your other fingers underneath.

2 Lift off the hat, turning it between your fingers and thumbs as you bring it in front of you.

3 Add a little flourish to your performance – casually cross one foot over the other as the hat reaches waist level.

Gentleperson JUGGLER

"Gentleman" for boys and "gentlewomen" for girls!

★ *Practice balancing a cane on your finger. Keep your finger underneath the tip of the cane. If the cane moves, move your finger with it. When you balance the cane on your chin, focus your eyes on the top of the cane. When the top of the cane moves, move so that your chin remains directly underneath the tip of the cane.*

A gentleperson's introduction

1 Enter with a swagger, holding your case, your cane, and your hat.

2 Greet the audience with a hat routine *(see pages 20-21)* and cane routine *(see page 19).*

★ *For a gentleperson's costume you will need a top hat; white gloves; a white T-shirt; a vest; a bow tie; a cane; and a small case for your juggling props (balls and scarves).*

3 Balance the inside of your hat on your cane. Balance the cane and hat on your chin.

4 Hold the base of the cane. Move it upward so that the hat flies up from the cane. Quickly move the cane to the side – and catch the hat on your head.

Take a break!

Place several colored scarves or handkerchiefs inside your hat – don't let the audience see this.

1 Enter wearing your hat. Take it off. Remove one scarf from your hat. Wipe your brow with the scarf as if you are tired or a little hot.

2 As you put your scarf back in your hat pretend to "find" some more scarves.

✔ *For a bold performance, exaggerate your movements and facial expressions.*

✔ *Add some comedy to your routine – clumsily open your case so your props fall out.*

3 Perform a juggling routine with your scarves.

4 Take out your juggling balls from your case and perform another excellent routine.

5 Roll up your gloves into two tight balls. Juggle with your gloves and your hat – spin it from its brim like a club.

6 For a spectacular finale to your routine, juggle with both of your gloves in one hand – catch them with your hat in your other hand.

The JESTER

You must be joking!

★ *For your hat you will need two differently colored pieces of felt or velvet, 8 inch wide and long enough to wrap over halfway around your head; a strip of material 1 inch wide and long enough to fit around your head; glue; scissors; needle and thread; and small metal bells (available from craft stores).*

Wear leggings and a T-shirt in bright colors.

1 From each 8 inch piece of material, cut out a crown shape, with 3 "peaks."

2 Hold the pieces around your head so that they fit together comfortably. Ask an adult to mark the material where the edges overlap.

3 Take the pieces off your head. Glue or sew the edges together as marked. Glue the tops of the peaks together.

4 Sew the strip of material around the bottom of your hat. Sew some bells onto the tops of the peaks.

Bubbling JUGGLING

Are you juggling with bubbles or balls?

★ *You will need: three transparent juggling balls (available from toy stores); bubble-blowing mixture; and a small case.*

1 Put the transparent balls in your case – leave the case open.

2 Dip the plastic wand in the bubble mixture. Blow on the wand to create some bubbles.

2 Pretend to catch three bubbles. Put them in the case.

3 Take out the transparent balls. Juggle them in a cascade. Your audience will think you are magically juggling three bubbles.

✔ *The jester can be a comic character. Juggle your balls as if they are a bit out of control.*

1

2

3

Fabulous food JUGGLING

Juggle with a potato, an onion, and an apple!

★ *Make a "bladder," a traditional jester's prop, out of a balloon taped to a stick* (left).

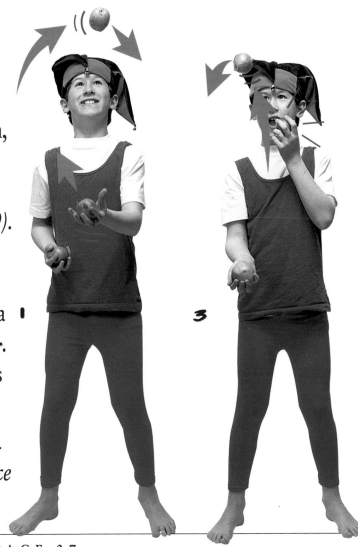

1 Juggle a potato, onion, and apple in a three-ball cascade.

2 Take the potato and onion into a two-ball one-handed circle *(see page 9)*.

3 Grasp the apple in your other hand. Take a bite out of it.

4 Bring the bitten apple back into a three-ball cascade. Repeat steps **2-4**. The problem of this trick increases as the apple gradually gets smaller!

✔ *Don't talk with your mouth full – unless you want to make the audience laugh! Yuk!*

JUGGLING *with* OTHERS

Share (or steal) your juggling with a friend.

"Stealing" between friends.

1 Your partner begins juggling a three-ball cascade.

2 Reach across your partner. With your inside arm, steal the ball that is farthest away from you.

3 Take the ball that is nearest to you with your outside arm.

4 Allow your partner to throw the last ball inside your arms in the cascade pattern. Steal that ball to complete your catch. Well done – you have now stolen all three balls! Begin a three-ball cascade.

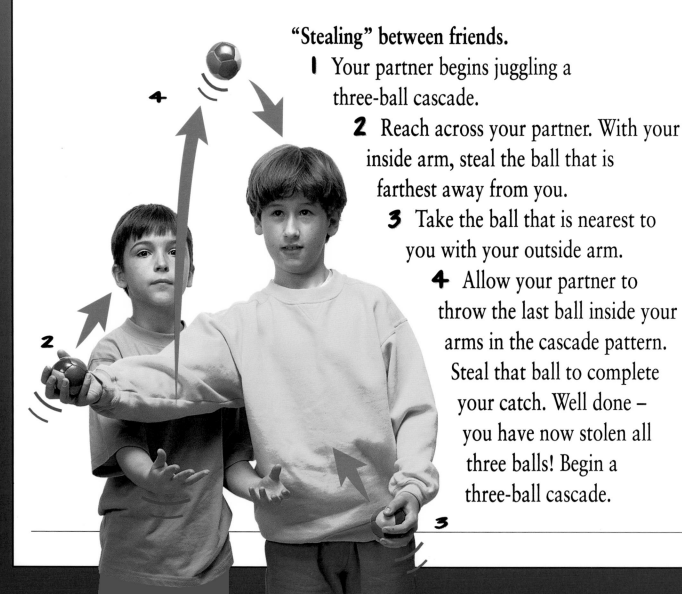

✔ *When you are performing in front of an audience, if you drop a juggling ball or club – don't worry! It happens to even the most experienced jugglers. There are plenty of ways to cover up a mistake – turn over the page for some ideas.*

6

5 As you are now juggling the three-ball cascade, your partner puts his or her inside arm around you and catches one ball. Put your inside arm around your partner.

6 You both juggle the three balls between you, with your outside arms.

7 On an agreed signal, your partner resumes juggling all three balls.

8 Now try this with clubs!

✔ *Stand opposite your partner. Your partner juggles a three-ball cascade. One by one, steal the three balls and begin a three-ball cascade. Try to juggle the three-ball cascade between you (left).*

Perfecting your ACT

Add a little extra to your performance.

Create a character

Choose an image or character for your
juggler. Adapt your routines to match the character. If you are
sharing your act *(see pages 28-29)*, dress as different
characters. Act the parts – for instance, as a jester
you could entertain a king or queen; teach the
king or queen how to juggle; then
perform as a double-act.

★ *These clowns* (right) *make a great
clown double-act. Make some costumes out of old
clothes – and lots of imagination.*

Putting your act together

1 Begin with the easiest tricks. Gradually introduce more
difficult tricks.

2 Spend about 10 seconds on each trick. Stop for applause –
and to catch your breath.

3 Write an amusing commentary, or patter, to accompany your trick or perform silently, to music. Play some music on a tape that will add to the atmosphere.

Cover up those mistakes!

Talk through your act. Patter is useful to cover any drops you may make. For example say, "This act is really picking up," or, "Oh dear, there was a sudden gust of gravity" as you retrieve your dropped objects. Shout "Look over there!" and point away from the audience – as they turn to look away, quickly pick up your prop and resume your juggling as if nothing has happened. Or quickly pick up your dropped object, continue juggling and say, "Good. Nobody noticed!"

✔ *Use actions to cover up any mistakes. If your character is foolish, such as the jester, go to pick up a dropped object, with another prop in your hand. Then drop that prop deliberately to make your pickup. Pretend to be surprised that there is still an object on the floor. Repeat the move several times.*

GLOSSARY

Cascade A basic figure eight juggling pattern.

Columns Two balls in one hand going up and down in straight lines.

Double-act Two people performing a routine.

Inside The path of a ball when it is thrown inside another ball.

Outside The path of a ball when it is thrown outside another ball.

Patter Some witty words to say during your act.

Peak The top height that a ball reaches when thrown.

Props The objects you juggle with.

INDEX

What to do NEXT

If you would like to take your juggling a step further, contact the International Jugglers Association, P.O. Box 218, Montague, Massachusetts, 01351. Tel: (413) 367-2401

All photos by Roger Vlitos except for page 3 – Mary Evans Picture Library. Models supplied from the Young People's Programme at Circus Space, Coronet Street, London N1
Tel: 0171 613 4141.